INTRODUCTION

In the 1980s it was decided that Penistone Road needed widening. What already seemed a wide enough road became a dual carriageway for the expanding volume of traffic that was to be expected - correctly as it turned out. In addition, Hillsborough Barracks was to become a major shopping centre with a variety of retail outlets including the massive Morrison's supermarket. Also, Supertram would need to have Langsett and Infirmary Roads more or less to itself so its traffic was diverted onto Penistone Road. The result has been traffic jams of irritating density during rush hours.

In order to bring this about extensive demolitions took place. On the eastern side most of the houses that made up small communities were completely demolished - in one instance to provide a site for the new Leisure Centre and swimming baths. Houses on the western side - notably those below Hillsborough Park escaped except those nearest to Penistone Road. They had to go and the following pages will show what they had looked like before the motor car became king.

In this book I have tried to show what the area was like during the first sixty years or so of my lifetime. I particularly remember the muck and magic of the Penistone Road of my childhood with the horses and carts, trams and buses, real motor cars - not the "cars" of today. In my youth "cars" were tramcars. The number of people who had a motor car was negligible. When I was at Malin Bridge School in the 1930s only one child was brought to school by car and that was in an Austin 7.

I have called the book an Owlerton Camera. Owlerton was an ancient manor and had its own manor house (see page 60). For the purposes of this book I have defined the area as stretching from the Wadsley Bridge at Penistone Road North along Penistone Road as far as Hillfoot Bridge. In addition I have taken in the hinterland to the east as far as the Five Arches and Wardsend.

Some may argue about the area but there is bound to be overlap between one area and another.

In any case I hope you will enjoy the pictures as much as I enjoyed taking them. It is amazing how quickly things change in this city of ours - now you see it; now you don't!!

This is my fifth book in the "Camera" series. I hope you like it.

INDEX

I took this photograph in 1970. On my way home I spotted demolition men about to demolish a chimney on land that is now Kilner Way. I was alarmed for the men who were nibbling away at the foundation of the chimney. I think Fred Dibnah earns every penny when felling such giants as this.

This train has just crossed Wadsley Bridge after passing the station on its way to Sheffield Victoria. On the left of the picture are the steel works of Moss and Gamble Brothers.
The date is around 1900.

MOSS & GAMBLE BROS.

Following the 1974 F.A. Cup semi-final at Hillsborough it was the police's duty to see the fans safely out of the city and at that time Wadsley Bridge station was still available.
These homeward bound Newcastle United supporters appeared happy enough, probably because they had just beaten Burnley 2-0, both goals scored by Supermac (Malcolm Macdonald)

Wadsley Bridge railway station was quite a pleasant little station but fell into disuse with the rise of the motor car and improved transport into Sheffield. Before the last war it would have been a pleasant country station for walkers heading for Southey or Fox Hill. It closed some years ago except for the odd occasion such as the one shown on the previous page.

This cementation furnace stood near the junction of Penistone Road North and Fox Hill Road. It is an old photograph but signs of abandonment are already present.

This is not one of mine but a much older photograph showing the shops and houses below the Wadsley railway bridge. It is difficult to put a date to this - but an old one.

The location on Penistone Road North is about the same as for the previous picture. The coal wagon is being followed by a tip horse (just visible at the rear of the cart) to assist on steep hills - and there are plenty of those in Sheffield. Notice the war memorial which means that the photograph probably dates from the 1920s.

Penistone Road North showing the Travellers pub as it was in 1958. At the time it was owned and used by Law Brothers for coach trips and the forecourt would be quite busy on Saturdays with holiday-makers going and coming.

The travellers pub at a later date following the demolition of most of the outbuildings and in preparation for the widening of the road.

Below the Travellers stood the old Gate pub seen here on the left. Across the road was a Methodist Chapel. The Gate has been replaced with a modern pub and the chapel has been demolished. And, of course, the old red phone box had to go.
See page 43 for a colour photograph of this public house

Take a look from the other side of the old Gate car park. On the left is Carmyles garage where I bought my Vauxhall Victor and had to push my part-exchange in on its last hundred yards. On the right the Fina garage is now the Carphone Warehouse and beyond was a really old building that also had to go. The shops beyond that were replaced with a drive-in take-away - more Americanisation.

A final look up Penistone Road North. The original Gate pub can be seen on the left with the lamp on the wall.

These cottages on Claywheels Lane survived until the 1950s. They look very picturesque but must have been uncomfortable to live in. The idyllic rural scene has now been swept away and the lane has become quite a busy thoroughfare. I doubt that a photographer could set up his tripod now with any safety.

These industrial premises near Claywheels Lane were photographed in 1974. My directory for the year suggests that this was either Niagara Forge or Dunford Hadfields Claywheels Rolling Mills.

This view was opposite the end of Clay Wheels Lane in 1981. The site is now occupied by the Hillfoot Steel Group.

The end of Leppings Lane in 1927. This cottage survived until the 1960s.

I noticed recently that the plot of land on Leppings Lane where these cottages stood is now being developed after being in use for some rather ramshackle garages for many years. Whatever takes their place can surely not be as attractive as these cottages. I give this photo a tentative date of 1908. (August 2004 - a block of flats are rising on this site).

An interesting view down Leppings Lane on match day. On the right is Law Brothers Filling station with petrol at 79p a gallon - no litres in those days and we knew what we were being charged. Now you would be lucky to get a litre for that price (which I understand is just over a pint and a half). When did you last see a policeman in a white coat? The date of this one is 1977.

Cup fever at the Wednesday ground as crowds head towards the ground. I was standing on Herries Road North when I took this photograph on 23rd April 1977. The 16 flagposts (one for each nation) had survived from 1966 World Cup when the ground was used for group matches and a quarter-final. One of the games was West Germany v Switzerland, a game which saw a young Franz Beckenbaur burst upon the football world stage.

This used to be a familiar site on match days. The tram "specials" waiting on Parkside Road to take the supporters back into the city after the match. Half an hour after the final whistle everybody was away.

Under siege. This newagent was taking no chances with a pent-up cup semi-final crowd. This photograph was taken on the same day as the picture on page 21.

An unusual view of the Five Arches on Herries Road showing the electrified line to Manchester while it was still in operation. The date is 1970. Since then much of the green space has been used for housing and the railway line is used only occasionally for the odd goods train. The valley to the lower right is Oxspring Valley.

FA Cup Semi-Final day at
Hillsborough on 23rd April 1977

This is 1924 and the constructors are busy building the new Herries Road. The cottage on the right has survived and is still to be seen nestling below the Five Arches. Thousands of Wednesday supporters were to tramp this new road on their way to "the match" after the New Parson Cross estate was completed.

This is the result of the activity shown on the previous page with Herries Road and Herries Road North laid out before us. To the left the Wednesday Ground is just visible. Most of the buildings shown have now been replaced. The date is 1970.

This view of Penistone Road from Parkside Road shows the location of Bastock Road. The large advertising board shows the road (see the next picture)

Bastock Road is the most northerly of the group of streets clustered opposite Hillsborough Park. I got this snap in 1982 before the houses disappeared.

Tanfield Road is a few yards nearer to Sheffield but on the same side as Bastock Road. It is now a small industrial development with no indication that it was once a thriving little community. My own mother lived here shortly before the First World War after marrying a soldier from the barracks.

These backs belonged to houses that faced Hillsborough Park (see the next page).

Match day at the Wednesday ground. Spectators on the right are passing the houses on Penistone Road whose backs were shown on the previous photograph. On the left is Hillsborough Park.

Another unique photograph of mounted cavalry returning to barracks and passing the very houses shown on the previous photograph. Shall we say 1900 - well my guess is as good as yours.

Penistone Road with Dutton Road on the right. Everything has gone here. To the left would be Parkside Road.

Dutton Road was situated opposite the bottom gates of Hillsborough Park across Penistone Road. It was one of a group of roads demolished to build the Leisure Centre.

Grant Road with Beulah Road in the distance. Bathers and other health-seekers now enjoy themselves on this plot.

You will find Beulah Road still there today but completely different to this photograph taken before all this was cleared to make way for Hillsborough Leisure Centre. This is now the road that leads to the entrance of the centre and also to the Bassett factory.

Here I am standing on Beulah Road. Beulah Rd had others that ran across where the Leisure Centre is. The nearer is Grant Road, then Harewood Road and Lofthouse Road. In the distance is the entrance to the Bassett factory.

GRANT ROAD

FISH CHIPS

RET 130 M

This section of Penistone Road between Broughton Road and Burnell Road all had to go for road widening. The pub is the Victoria that stood at the bottom of Burrowlee Road.

Lily's sandwich shop at the corner of Burrowlee Road now occupies much grander premises than it did when this photograph was taken. All the shops on the right were demolished and a new shop for Lily was built farther back. (see page 49)

A view of Herries Road North. The Corporation bus depot can be seen and also the shops lately demolished to create a Burger King drive-in fast food outlet. Taken in 1980. Top left is the Niagra Sports Ground owned by the South Yorkshire Police Force.

Here are some things to jog your memory. The view shows the end of Bradfield Road with the Royal Hotel prominent. Across Bradfield Road was Hillfoot Steel. The Barracks are behind in all their muck. I got this shot with a telephoto lens shooting over Owlerton Stadium. The blue thing bottom left is a pylon insulator that got in the way. Kentucky Fried Chickens has replaced the Royal Hotel. The date was 1980.

The Gate pub was demolished and a new one built in its place. It stood above Claywheels Lane. See page 12 There was an even earlier pub on the site, see page14. This photo dates from 1974.

This was Wardsend Cemetery as it was in 1968 - very much neglected and far from the beauty spot it had once been when the area was a favoured country walk. If you ever get the chance take a look at the view of Owlerton that used to be in the Museum with sheep grazing on what is now Owlerton Stadium but was then the village green.

The road that curves around the Gasometer was Farfield Road - there is a pub of the same name. The straighter road to the right was Hoyland Road. Note the outside privvies and the back alley between. The road visible centre right is Wood Street leading up to Langsett Road. St. Bartholomew's Chapel on Burgoyne Road can be seen on the right of the frame. The photograph dates from 1968.

This was taken quite recently by following a footpath from Penrith Road when this view was suddenly exposed. I was looking towards Owlerton Stadium and beyond to Bradfield Road flats on the right and Hillsborough Barracks on the left.

The Old Crown at No. 710 Penistone Road is clearly of two periods. The white front is the older and must have seen many changes. When it was built it would have been a country pub. Around 1900 the red brick part would have been added.

Across Sedgley Road from the Old Crown stands Owlerton Church - the church of St. John the Baptist. The church is not that old as churches go but one of the few evangelising churches with its wayside pulpit. My mother and father were married here and I have a photo of my Uncle Joe, who was a Sunday School teacher at the church, with a group of young churchgoers. Uncle Joe was killed on the first day of the Somme 1916.

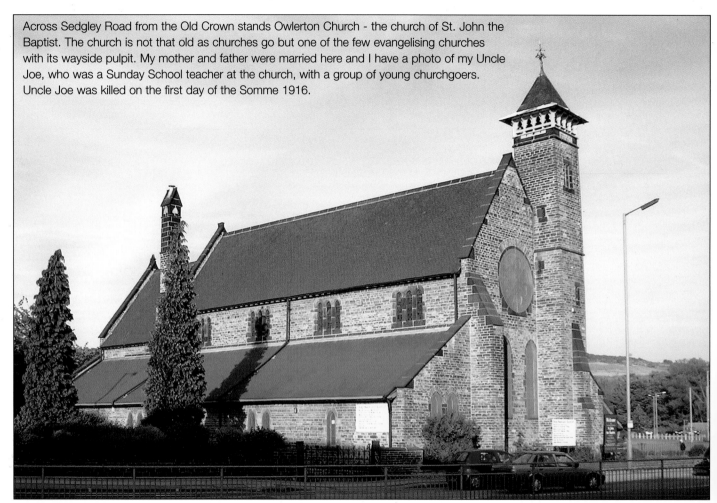

Lily's new shop is here seen under construction and nearing completion. The date is 11th March 1986. On the right is Burrowlee Road with just a glimpse of the Victoria pub.

The Victoria pub was a fine Victorian pub at the corner of Penistone Road and Burrowlee Road. When this photograph was taken on 11th March 1986 its days were numbered. When I returned a week or two later it had been fired and the charred roof timbers were exposed. Thereafter it was demolished..

Taken from Broughton Road this shows the backyards of houses on Penistone Road that have now gone.

A wide view of Owlerton as it was in 1970. The Wednesday Ground is to the right and Hillsborough Park to the left. Many of the lost houses that feature in this book are visible. Notice the acres of vacant land in the foreground.

These two shops situated between Burnell road and Borough Road were to be demolished as was the little garden beyond. I was amazed later to see people digging up plants from the garden and rather angry until I realised that they were saving the snowdrops, daffodils, shrubs and alpines from the bulldozer. Extract from The Star (11 Apr 1986) ...the shop, W.A. Buckley and Son has been run by members of the family for 55 years... It was first opened in 1930... Ray Glover, the baker next door, said "we have worked together for 27 years and never a cross word. It has been a pleasure working with Mr. Buckley. Ray Buckley, the son, decided it was time to retire. The photo was taken on 22 March 1986.

This view was taken in 1970. The block of houses centre right were all demolished and Hillsborough Leisure Centre now occupies the site opposite Hillsborough Park. In the centre is Bassetts Sweet factory.

Soldiers from Hillsborough Barracks in camp on Birley Meadows. The date is around 1900. In the distance can be seen industrial Sheffield. This and the other early photographs relating to Hillsborough Barracks were sold to me by a descendant of the photographer and have never been seen before. There is a dearth of photographs showing life at the barracks.

Here again is Birley
Meadows but this time
with the Horse Artillery
lined up - probably for
inspection.

Taken from the top storey of Bradfield Road flats this view from the early 1980s shows Hillfoot Steel on the right and on the left the Sportsman's Group pub (see the next page) both of which were to be demolished when the road became dual carriageway.

The Sportsman's Group public house at 851 Penistone Road. The origin of the name is unknown but it probably stems from the fact that people used to gather in groups to watch bare knuckle fights, potty rise, and other sporting events take place on the land adjacent.

Penistone Road showing the houses and shops that stood opposite Hillsborough Park as they were in 1982. All these buildings have now disappeared.

Owlerton Manor was situated between Bradfield Road and Owlerton Green with its back to Penistone Road opposite Owlerton Stadium. The building dated from Elizabethan times. Notice the spy-hole in the front gable. It was demolished in 1931

Owlerton Bridge on Penistone Road near to Livesey Street as it was in 1986 before the road became dual carriageway. The building is Pearson's Forge.

This was how the barracks looked in the days before B&Q. That beautiful wall enclosed a large plot of land (now B&Q car park) that bordered the River Loxley. I remember as a child watching a football game played there but that would have been after the barracks had been sold off.

I obtained this postcard on the E Bay auction site. The inscription on the back reads: N.C.O's "F" block. Married Quarters, Hillsborough Barracks. Sheffield. Taken by Lieut. Smith. Novr. 1914. I wonder how many of these fine young men survived the First World War.

This is how the B&Q site looked before Morrison's took over. I am not sure whether the vans were for sale or just parked. 26th April 1986 was the date.

Near to the Barracks two pubs faced each other. The older was the Cambridge (right). It was damaged by the Sheffield Flood of 1864. Rose Inn on the left was Victorian and was used as a mortuary when that great disaster hit Sheffield. Both have now been demolished. (Details from "Sheffield Public Houses" by Michael Liversidge.)

This is a clearer picture of the Rose Inn than on the previous page. It was recently been demolished after a determined effort by the Historic Society of Bradfield to save it failed.
It was also a fine example of a Garrison pub, which was a watering hole built in the first instance to supply drinks for the soldiers of the Hillsborough Barracks.

Next to the Barracks on the Sheffield side were these industrial buildings belonging to C.G. Carlisle & Co., steel manufacturers. It has now been swept away and another MacDonald's has taken its place. The date was 26th April 1986.

The New Barrack Tavern, on Penistone Road, is still open but without the little shop that was attached when I took this photograph in 1988.

Following the demolition of the surrounding houses there came a good view of Burton Street brewery. I noticed on a recent visit that the noble chimney had been truncated.

The road to the right is Wood Grove Road and across Penistone Road is
Hobson Avenue. The date of this is 1970.
The factory belonged to Easterbrook and Allcard.

A view of Penistone Road from the bottom of Fawley Road.

This row of shops stood between Cottam
Street and Driffield St. They were known
as the ABCD streets - that is Anlaby,
Brough, Cottam and Driffield.
This photograph dates from 1968.

This takes you around the corner onto Cottam Street and shows the back yard behind the shops where I used to play while my mother helped her sister in the shop - usually on Fridays which was the busy time after workers had been paid. I remember they has a collie dog called Peter - very street wise, well it had to be living on busy Penistone Road.

Looking down from Bamforth Street towards the works of Annealers Ltd. on the left. Buildings on the right were demolished and the site is now occupied by Monty's Motors. The electric power station is top right.

A view from Cuthbert Bank towards Hillfoot Bridge as it looked in 1970. The houses were on Hicks Road and Grove Square. The area was heavily industrial.

Old Park Silver Mill is situated on Club Mill Road.
This photograph was taken in 1974.

Wood Street is opposite Hillfoot Bridge but is now nothing like this picture taken in 1968.

CAPSTAN

PARK DRIVE

A look back from Hillfoot Bridge towards Cuthbert Bank. The date was 17th February 1968. The houses at the very top were on Langsett Road. The lonely pair of semis had not much longer to go.

This was taken in 1968 looking across Hillfoot Bridge to the Farfield pub. For a view of the area from a different direction see the next page.

For my last picture I could not resist this one although it encroaches on Neepsend. It continues the previous picture so well that it is almost panoramic. Needless to say it was taken at the same time.